REJECTION

IS A

BLESSING

HOW TO DEAL WITH AND OVERCOME REJECTION

Re'Dina L. Frazier

To order additional copies of this book, contact:
Xlibris
1-888-795-4274
www.Xlibris.com
Orders@Xlibris.com

ISBN: Softcover   978-1-7960-9544-9
       EBook   978-1-7960-9543-2

Designed by Freepik

Print information available on the last page

Rev. date: 03/20/2020

First of all, let's get the realness of it all out of the way. Rejection hurts. Rejection sucks. Rejection is something no one wants to face because of the feeling that comes behind the actual dismissal. When someone dismisses us from their life - the first thing we think is that we're not good enough. This thought of being not good enough can bring about an array of emotions for some people. Having the feeling of not measuring up to a person, and or task (as in employment) can make us think that we're not suitable enough and can cause us to question our own existence.

re·jec·tion
/rəˈjekSH(ə)n/

noun
the dismissing or refusing of a proposal, idea, etc.
"the Union decided last night to recommend rejection of the offer"

Similar:
refusal
nonacceptance
declining
turning down
no
dismissal
spurning
rebuff
knock-back
repudiation
abandonment
forsaking
desertion
shutting out
exclusion
shunning
cold-shouldering
ostracizing
ostracism
blackballing
blacklisting
avoidance
ignoring

snubbing

snub

cutting dead

sending to Coventry

brush-off

a kick in the teeth

excommunication

the spurning of a person's affections.

However anyone describes it - rejection is the one thing every ego fears.

There are those who internalize a situation and those who externalize a situation. Both, if not dealt with properly and with sound judgment could lead to self destruction.

in·ter·nal·ize
/inˈtərnlˌīz/

Learn to pronounce

verb

1.
PSYCHOLOGY
make (attitudes or behavior) part of one's nature by learning or unconscious assimilation.

Whenever we internalize unwanted circumstances that come up in our lives we're placing an unnecessary weight onto ourselves. And, the more we hold it in the heavier that weight becomes. The only way to rid ourselves of the additional mental weight is by the process of eliminating it from our lives. We can do this by journaling our thoughts, or writing them down on paper and burning it, or speaking to someone about it. Internalizing our true feelings whenever we're hurting inside is like repeatedly falling on daggers willingly. We are only doing damage to ourselves whenever we refuse help.

ex·ter·nal·ize
/ikˈstərnəˌlīz/

verb
give external existence or form to.

express (a thought or feeling) in words or actions.

PSYCHOLOGY
project (a mental image or process) onto a figure outside oneself.

Whenever we externalize (if done with a sound mind) we're better able to gain clarity of a matter. Speaking about it frees our mind and gives our soul permission to move past the current situation. But, if we externalize in a way that's far too extreme (dramatically speaking) it could start a whirlwind of unfortunate events. When we're being extra, nothing good ever comes from it. It can only make whatever is going on much worse.

Hopefully, when faced with rejection we choose a mentally stable way of dealing with it - a way that doesn't call for bail money, a rubber room, or a well lined expensive casket.

CONTENTS

CHAPTER 1

PARENTAL RELATED REJECTION

It all starts at home. Everything that we'll ever face in life - love, indifference, friendship, betrayal, acceptance, heartache and yes, rejection all starts with those in our home who are supposed to mean the most to us. Or, of whom, we're supposed to mean the most to.

Our first love affair is with our parents. The two people who came together in love and created us. Unfortunately, parents are not exempt from being the very ones who reject us, or dismiss our very existence.

There are many reasons why a parent, cling to a favorite child and avoid another one. Or, why a parent pushes their child away altogether. Some parents may cling to one child because they remind them of a time when they were most happy, or in love with a certain person. Some parents may show indifference to one child because they regret ever knowing (in the biblical sense) the partner of which they had that particular child with. And, some parents show indifference towards all of their children because they may feel trapped, scared, lonely or confused - being thrust into parenthood before they could begin their own lives.

Rejection from a parent, or guardian is the hardest thing a child could ever go through, because the rejection is coming from someone whose love should be unconditional. The one person on planet earth who's supposed to rally around them and support them in all your positive endeavors.

When a parent rejects their child, it's felt and seen as hatred. Dismissal from a parent can ultimately destroy a child mentally, emotionally, physically and spiritually.

Mentally because it does psychological damage that can last a lifetime and no doubt effect how that child interacts with people around them. Whereby, they may become a introvert, or extrovert. Either pulling away from people because of fear of rejection, or becoming loud and boisterous in order to be heard and seen. Sadly, the later is a over compensation for the lack of attention they receive from their parents, or guardian. In this case, the loudest in the room is the weakest in the room.

Emotionally because it can make us weak, susceptible to the many toxic inhumane treatments of others. Forever trying to fit in with things and people we have no business being around. Ever trying to seek the approval of people who are beneath our level of understanding. Not that we're all that, but we know who we are and who we were meant to be. Some people, aren't deserving of you. And, when you're vulnerable the many traps of life can entangle you.

Physically because, if we allow it, our health can take a nosedive. Some people eat their feelings. Some people take on risky tasks, or assignments to prove themselves to their parents - like saying, "Ma, look at me, see I told you I could do it". Meanwhile, the parent in question isn't even looking in their direction. Dreadfully so, some people give up on themselves altogether when they see that they'll never win the heart of their parent/s. Even their appearence and hygiene suffers as a result. It all stems from a lack of parental love, or support.

Spiritually because, parental dismissal cuts to the soul of a person. It can break you like nothing else, or no one ever can. When our soul is destroyed by the people who we love the most, it can make one a mere shell of themselves - only existing and not living. Our spirit man (the heart of who we are) slowly dies and we can become walking zombies. We're talking, walking around, laughing, mingling with people, but we're dead inside. It can be especially painful whenever you witness your parents giving the love, respect and support that you so desperately want to total strangers. It's kind of satan's way of twisting the knife that's already in your ribs - that your parents placed there.

Luke 12:53 King James Version (KJV)

53 The father shall be divided against the son, and the son against the father; the mother

against the daughter, and the daughter against the mother; the mother in law against her daughter in law, and the daughter in law against her mother in law.

Truth is, we live in a world where people are more engrossed in themselves than their priorities.

Father's abandon their children on a regular basis. For some, it's to find greener pastures. For some, it's because the wives/homie/lovers/friends were too nagging and controlling. For some, it was because they were little boys trapped in grown men bodies, not ready to take on real life responsibilities. Some just die. Whatever the reason, for the sake of amusement, we'll say that they simply went out to get a pack cigarettes and forgot their way back home.

Whenever a Father chooses to abandon their children, those children are left to pick up the pieces and mend not only themselves back to health, but their Mother's as well.

For boys, that young man has a difficult time becoming a man, because he never experienced what a real man is - unless he was fortunate enough to have a strong male role model in his life to help guide him along his path. For those who have fallen by the wayside, their lives can take traumatic turns that could potentially lead to incarceration, or the grave - only if no one steps up to stand in the gap.

For girls, it's a downward spiral that can lead to mistrust, anger issues, unbalanced submissiveness, controlling behavior, or even promiscuity. Girls who are looking for their father's love seek it in the wrong faces and places. Men who prey on "Lost Girls" can smell these troubled souls a half mile away. These hurt little girls are encased in grown women bodies and the filthy slim of the land take advantage of their vulnerable nature. And, in a warped sense, become these little girls who are lost Father figure. It's not until she realizes that the love she's been looking for all of her life she had all along - and that love was/is that of the ultimate Father - Abba Father.

Mother's, for whatever reason, start tripping on some whacked out mess from their past that they can't seem to shake - so everyone in their immediate vicinity feels the wrath of Genghis Khan, unless there is a favorite child who can do no wrong in her eyes. But, to stay on topic, some Mother's (the ones who remain) abandon their children by not being there for them, or supporting them, or protecting them. Children, no matter the age, can feel when the love isn't being returned. A Mother's love is really all children need to be successful in life. When that love isn't reciprocated, it can do soulish damage to that child.

For boy's, the void of a Mother's love can force a young underdeveloped mind to seek comfort from other women. In this case, pornography via magazines, or the web can be used to fill the gap. Some seek the service of "paid women" in order to fill the gap. For these type of boys/men - it's not about having hidden desires for their mother's, it's about being held, feeling needed and respected - even if it's a temporary fix. In some instances, boys trapped in men bodies can take to unwelcome sexual acts - not for the release at the end, but as a way to gain some kind of control over a woman. And some, howbeit rare, resort to the whole Norman Bates way of thinking. Yes, there are men who kill and mummify their Mother's and live as their mother, because they believe that they can be a better mother. The above mentioned is not always the case, especially if the boys have a mother figure, such as a Big Mama, or Aunt to step into that void. Some men, go on to become successful leaders and great role models.

For girls, well let's just say, it's not a very pleasant household to grow up in. Women, no matter the relationship, have always been at odds with one another. The excessive eye rolling, quiet slamming of the doors, stepping on every crack while walking home from school hoping her back would be broken before you arrived, seemingly talking to, or dating all the wrong types - that somehow manage to make your mother's blood boil every time. Or, simply breathing in a common area. With daughters and mothers, there are no hidden woes, or agendas. Women have always managed to let the other know exactly how they feel.

en·mi·ty
/ˈenmədē/

noun
the state or feeling of being actively opposed or hostile to someone or something.

A woman can ask, or begged another woman to do something and when it's done, exactly as requested - the one doing the asking will still find fault and be sore displeased.

Then Sarai said to Abram, "My wrong be upon you! I gave my maid into your embrace; and when she saw that she had conceived, I became despised in her eyes. The LORD judge between you and me."

Although Sarai/Sarah asked her hand maiden to accept her husband unto herself, Sarah became envious of Hagar. And likewise, Hagar became jealous of Sarah. Let's just say, Sarah screwed up, big time, it did not go the way she'd like. In the end, Sarah confessed, «My bad, Dawg".

Look, all I'm saying is, there's nothing new under the sun. Women have always saw another woman as competition, or a threat - even mothers. For the most part, the daughters move away and begin a life of their own - far far far away from their mother's. Although Hagar wasn't Sarah's daughter, she was in close quarters with her. Hagar got the heck on into Never Neverland - 'til this day, 2020, the two regions are still fighting because of what happened between Sarah and Hagar. The war between Isaac and Ishmael will continue until the end of the world.

CHAPTER 2

SIBLING RELATED REJECTION

Yes. Siblings are capable of being apart of that unwanted group of people who feel the need to dismiss us. This type of dismissal goes far beyond sibling rivalry. If you have a sibling, or someone who you grew up with that served as a sibling in your life, such as a cousin, or uncle/aunt around your same age, at some point discord among you has reared its ugly head.

Sibling rivalry is a type of competition or animosity among siblings, whether blood-related or not.

This, however, is not that. This is about one sibling who refuses to accept the other as a blood relative. This thought process usually occurs when one of the siblings sense the vibes of a parent, or someone who has guardianship over the siblings that has shown partiality towards a favorite child and animosity towards another. Children can not only pick up the vibes around them, but actually can take on those vibes and start exhibiting the same behavior. The sibling who is holding onto the unfounded animosity usually puts their energy into causing strife and confusion between the parent and the sibling. Even going as far as to sabotage their sibling, or set them up to get into some kind of heated interaction with the parent. There is no love, or feelings of regret - they have most assuredly set themselves against their sibling.

Romans 9: 13 (KJV)
As it is written, Jacob have I loved, but Esau have I hated.

Genesis 27: 1-41; 42-45 (NET)
Jacob cheats Esau out of the blessing

27 When Isaac was old and his eyes were so weak that he was almost blind, he called his older son Esau and said to him, "My son!" "Here I am!" Esau replied. 2 Isaac said, "Since I am so old, I could die at any time.3 Therefore, take your weapons—your quiver and your bow—and go out into the open fields and hunt down some wild game for me. 4 Then prepare for me some tasty food, the kind I love, and bring it to me. Then I will eat it so that I may bless you before I die."

5 Now Rebekah had been listening while Isaac spoke to his son Esau. When Esau went out to the open fields to hunt down some wild game and bring it back, 6 Rebekah said to her son Jacob, "Look, I overheard your father tell your brother Esau, 7 'Bring me some wild game and prepare for me some tasty food. Then I will eat it and bless you in the presence of the Lord before I die.' 8 Now then, my son, do exactly what I tell you! 9 Go to the flock and get me two of the best young goats. I'll prepare them in a tasty way for your father, just the way he loves them. 10 Then you will take it to your father. Thus he will eat it and bless you before he dies."

11 "But Esau my brother is a hairy man," Jacob protested to his mother Rebekah, "and I have smooth skin! 12 My father may touch me! Then he'll think I'm mocking him and I'll bring a curse on myself instead of a blessing." 13 So his mother told him, "Any curse against you will fall on me, my son! Just obey me! Go and get them for me!"

14 So he went and got the goats and brought them to his mother. She prepared some tasty food, just the way his father loved it. 15 Then Rebekah took her older son Esau's best clothes, which she had with her in the house, and put them on her younger son Jacob. 16 She put the skins of the young goats on his hands and the smooth part of his neck. 17 Then she handed the tasty food and the bread she had made to her son Jacob.

18 He went to his father and said, "My father!" Isaac replied, "Here I am. Which are you, my son?" 19 Jacob said to his father, "I am Esau, your firstborn. I've done as you told me. Now sit up and eat some of my wild game so that you can bless me."20 But Isaac asked his son, "How in the world did you find it so quickly, my son?" "Because the Lord your God brought it to me," he replied. 21 Then Isaac said to Jacob, "Come closer so I can touch you, my son, and know for certain if you really are my son Esau." 22 So Jacob went over to his father Isaac, who felt him and said, "The voice is Jacob's, but the hands are Esau's." 23 He did not recognize him because his hands were hairy, like his brother Esau's hands. So Isaac blessed Jacob. 24 Then he asked, "Are you really my son Esau?" "I am," Jacob replied. 25 Isaac said, "Bring some of the wild game for me to eat, my son. Then I will bless you." So Jacob brought it to him, and he ate it. He also brought him wine, and Isaac drank. 26 Then his father Isaac said to him, "Come here and kiss me, my son." 27 So Jacob went over and kissed him. When Isaac caught the scent of his clothing, he blessed him, saying,

"Yes, my son smells
like the scent of an open field
which the Lord has blessed.
28 May God give you
the dew of the sky
and the richness of the earth,
and plenty of grain and new wine.
29 May peoples serve you
and nations bow down to you.
You will be lord over your brothers,
and the sons of your mother will bow down to you.
May those who curse you be cursed,
and those who bless you be blessed."

30 Isaac had just finished blessing Jacob, and Jacob had scarcely left his father's presence, when his brother Esau returned from the hunt. 31 He also prepared some tasty food and brought it to his father. Esau said to him, "My father, get up and eat some of your son's wild game. Then you can bless me." 32 His father Isaac asked, "Who are you?" "I am your firstborn son," he replied, "Esau!" 33 Isaac began to shake violently and asked, "Then who else hunted game and brought it to me? I ate all of it just before you arrived, and I blessed him. He will indeed be blessed!"

34 When Esau heard his father's words, he wailed loudly and bitterly. He said to his father, "Bless me too, my father!" 35 But Isaac replied, "Your brother came in here deceitfully

and took away your blessing." 36 Esau exclaimed, "Jacob is the right name for him! He has tripped me up two times! He took away my birthright, and now, look, he has taken away my blessing!" Then he asked, "Have you not kept back a blessing for me?"

37 Isaac replied to Esau, "Look! I have made him lord over you. I have made all his relatives his servants and provided him with grain and new wine. What is left that I can do for you, my son?" 38 Esau said to his father, "Do you have only that one blessing, my father? Bless me too!" Then Esau wept loudly.

39 So his father Isaac said to him,

"See here, your home will be by the richness of the earth,
and by the dew of the sky above.
40 You will live by your sword
but you will serve your brother.
When you grow restless,
you will tear off his yoke
from your neck."

41 So Esau hated Jacob because of the blessing his father had given to his brother. Esau said privately, "The time of mourning for my father is near; then I will kill my brother Jacob!"

43 Now then, my son, do what I say. Run away immediately to my brother Laban in Haran. 44 Live with him for a little while[cj] until your brother's rage subsides. 45 Stay there until your brother's anger against you subsides and he forgets what you did to him. Then I'll send someone to bring you back from there. Why should I lose both of you in one day?"

Clearly, this was much more than sibling rivalry - it was sheer hatred. Not only did one brother have very disturbing feelings towards the other, but their mother hated her own son, Esau as well.

Jacob rejected Esau on every turn, because he saw how much their mother loathed him.

CHAPTER 3

WORK
RELATED
REJECTION

In this dysfunctional world that we live in, there seems to always be someone who refuses to vibe with us, as wonderful of a person as we are. No matter how much you attempt to get along with this person - they, for some odd reason reject your efforts. We offer to stay late in order to help them catch up with their assignments - even though it means paying the babysitter a little extra. We bring them hot coffee in the morning - even though it means driving a few blocks out of the way. We leave peppermints on their desk - not thinking that they'll perceive it as a low - key diss. We acknowledge them on their birthday and holidays - even if they never acknowledge us. We even let them pick out their Krispy Kreme donuts first, that we bought for the entire office and hardly batted an eye when they picked out our favorites.

All of this labor of love to only have our sincere efforts fall on stony ground. It's easy to say, "bump ‹em", even easier to throw up the deuces and shake the dust. But, because we're from a different breed, we overlook their wicked behavior and pray for them, because we're a peculiar people - or, at least supposed to be. We're taught not to treat others the way they treat us. We're taught to exhibit kindness in the throes of unkindness. We're taught to be more like Jesus and less like Aunt Lucy. And, we all have a Aunt Lucy who doesn't care about hurting anyone's feelings as long as the truth is told. WWJD.

But, there are certain people who refuse to allow us to showcase our brotherly love. Some people won't allow peace to dwell within them, so they're not going to allow peace to reign between them and someone else. And by someone else, I mean YOU. These people picked you out as a target straight from the door. They sized you up and studied you long enough to find your weaknesses. They use what they have learned about you to attack you. See, while you were being Mother Teresa, from a sincere heart - they looked at that as your weakness. And that, my darling, is what they'll use to destroy you.

2 Samuel 11: 1-17; 27 New King James Version (*NKJV*)

David, Bathsheba, and Uriah

1 It happened in the spring of the year, at the time when kings go out to battle, that David sent Joab and his servants with him, and all Israel; and they destroyed the people of Ammon and besieged Rabbah. But David remained at Jerusalem.

2 Then it happened one evening that David arose from his bed and walked on the roof of the king's house. And from the roof he saw a woman bathing, and the woman was very beautiful to behold. 3 So David sent and inquired about the woman. And someone said, "Is this not Bathsheba, the daughter of Eliam, the wife of Uriah the Hittite?" 4 Then David sent messengers, and took her; and she came to him, and he lay with her, for she was cleansed from her impurity; and she returned to her house. 5 And the woman conceived; so she sent and told David, and said, "I am with child."

6 Then David sent to Joab, saying, "Send me Uriah the Hittite." And Joab sent Uriah to David. 7 When Uriah had come to him, David asked how Joab was doing, and how the people were doing, and how the war prospered. 8 And David said to Uriah, "Go down to your house and wash your feet." So Uriah departed from the king's house, and a gift of food from the king followed him. 9 But Uriah slept at the door of the king's house with all the servants of his lord, and did not go down to his house. 10 So when they told David, saying, "Uriah did

not go down to his house," David said to Uriah, "Did you not come from a journey? Why did you not go down to your house?"

11 And Uriah said to David, "The ark and Israel and Judah are dwelling in tents, and my lord Joab and the servants of my lord are encamped in the open fields. Shall I then go to my house to eat and drink, and to lie with my wife? As you live, and as your soul lives, I will not do this thing."

12 Then David said to Uriah, "Wait here today also, and tomorrow I will let you depart." So Uriah remained in Jerusalem that day and the next. 13 Now when David called him, he ate and drank before him; and he made him drunk. And at evening he went out to lie on his bed with the servants of his lord, but he did not go down to his house.

14 In the morning it happened that David wrote a letter to Joab and sent it by the hand of Uriah. 15 And he wrote in the letter, saying, "Set Uriah in the forefront of the hottest battle, and retreat from him, that he may be struck down and die." 16 So it was, while Joab besieged the city, that he assigned Uriah to a place where he knew there were valiant men. 17 Then the men of the city came out and fought with Joab. And some of the people of the servants of David fell; and Uriah the Hittite died also.

27 And when her mourning was over, David sent and brought her to his house, and she became his wife and bore him a son. But the thing that David had done displeased the Lord.

This passage of scriptures is a great example of not only rejection, but betrayal by someone in authority. Because of David's lust for Bathsheba, he orchestrated the murder of his servant, Uriah. This isn't to say that all accounts of rejection are to this extreme, but it does let us know that spiritual wickedness exist in the workplace. This is why it's best to make wise decisions when choosing our employers and coworkers. It's God (Yahweh) who opens doors - allow Him to lead you to the job/ career that's most suited for you and your earthly purpose.

CHAPTER 4

LOVE INTEREST REJECTION

Narcissistic people thrive on the pull and push away. You can spend months and even years dealing with one person only to hear them say "We're not in a relationship". In fact, it's the only sure thing about the non-relationship that you can bank on. But, you remain in your non-committal situationship hoping things change, but they seldom do.

These type of situationships only end up ushering in depression, a defeatist attitude and a contrite spirit. It can be challenging to give of yourself to someone consistently and in return receive nothing - absolutely no reciprocation. But, it's not like you haven't tried to walk away several times before. You've tried, but your empathetic nature led you right back into the devil's layer.

You know your worth and know that you're worth much more than you are receiving from the person who doesn't want to commit. You've had "The Talk" addressing the C word and they've made promises to change. Or, at some point, you›ve both decided to walk away only to find yourselves back in each other's arms.

You've given your all and have done everything you knew to do, but still it all remains the same. They talk a good game, pulling you back in and as soon as they see that you've opened up your heart back up to them again - they push you away - again. This is typical narcissistic behavior.

Narcissists are extremely selfish, lack empathy, thrive on attention and have a over exaggerated sense of self. They believe they are entitled to whatever, or whoever. They are takers, very controlling, arrogant and dangerous - on a psychotic level. Whenever a narcissist doesn't get their way they'll do whatever it takes to manipulate the situation in order to turn things in their favor - this includes lying, stealing, gossiping, revealing secrets - and even murder.

A Narcissist's only goal is to get what they want by any means necessary. They do not care who gets hurt in the process. Their heightened ability to careless is off the charts - even if someone's death is involved. A Narcissist will make it painfully clear that they are not the ones to rely on in times of crisis. Whenever you think of a person who is demonically possessed - look no further than a Narcissist.

A Narcissist will fake a relationship to keep the benefits from running out. This includes having children with the person, or even marrying them. To a Narcissist, the marriage license is just a piece of paper, it means nothing and holds no weight. Narcissists are capable of cheating on their spouse on their wedding night.

As long as you're complying with a Narcissist they're completely happy. But, the moment you say NO and mean it - you've just awakened Hell. Narcissist's egos are humongous. they can't handle anyone standing up for themselves and saying the word - NO.

Narcissist will use the silent treatment as a way to punish the people who grow the strength to stand up to them. Don't get it twisted though, although they may have you on palm mode, they are watching your every move. Narcissist are the inventors of stalking people. You are being watched by them and their flying monkeys - those who are of mutual acquaintance. And, if you decide to move on with your life - they will not only find out with who, they'll make underhanded moves to sabotage your new relationship - so expect to be lied on by your Narcissist - they play dirty. They are very deceptive and controlling.

The best way to beat a Narcissist at their own game is to drop off the face of the earth. Don't answer their calls, text, emails, doorbell rings/ knocks, or third, fourth, or fifth party contacts - who are only coming to you asking questions to report back to the Narcissist.

Go GHOST.

Change your name to Casper. Leave them alone for good. If you decide to return to a Narcissist, things between you will only be worse, because Narcissist love to make you pay for leaving them - they believe in revenge.

And, they'll make your life a living Hell.

These people have perfected rejection on a PhD level. When their love bombing tactics have won you over (again) - they'll flip the script and start dismissing you on every turn, nothing you do will please them. If you say right, they'll say left. If you choose white, they'll choose black. They'll side with anyone who opposes you. Trust, this is their innate wickedness attempting to annihilate you. This is apart of their strategy to break you down and rip out your soul. These people are evil - there is no good in them. Don't chase behind them - run as far away from them as you possibly can. Move to another city if you must. 1-800-468-4285 (U-Haul).

Warning: never inform a Narcissist of your plans - it'll bite you in the buns if you do. And if you marry one, you'll have to fight Hell and its dominions to get out of it.

CHAPTER 5

OVERCOMING HEARTACHE

Time to let it go.

Yes, it hurts. The memories of rejection is painful - it never goes away. We can't change the past - all we do is grow from it, blossoming into beautiful flowers that make the world a more amazing place to be in.

Okay, what Daddy did and Mama said still hunts you to this day. How your Boss, or Coworker treated you still stings and makes you feel some type of way. How your Significant Other made you feel when you were together made you a little bitter and apprehensive about dating again - ever.

But, you know what, you are not the person they made you out to be. Those people who hated you without a cause don't get to dictate how you should be living your life. They don't get a say so in the direction your life goes. Their words and actions towards you is their own karma. You didn't warrant their behavior towards you - they made conscious decisions to mismanage your relationship with them.

It's them who came out the loser, because they missed out on having someone who's a loving, caring, giving, loyal and overall wonderful person. See, in the end, you win, because you didn't allow their malevolent behavior to destroy you, or turn you into the same type of hideous creature.

So, now, the choice is yours - either you can continue to live in the past allowing the heartache and mental suffering to hold you captive. Or, you can press towards the mark of a higher calling. Leaving the past behind and high stepping into your joy - filled future.

John 10: 10 King James Version (KJV)

10 The thief cometh not, but for to steal, and to kill, and to destroy: I am come that they might have life, and that they might have it more abundantly.

CHAPTER 6

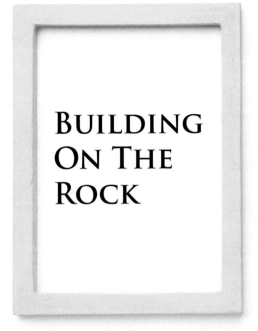

BUILDING ON THE ROCK

Matthew 16: 13-20 King James Version (KJV)

13 When Jesus came into the coasts of Caesarea Philippi, he asked his disciples, saying, Whom do men say that I the Son of man am?

14 And they said, Some say that thou art John the Baptist: some, Elias; and others, Jeremias, or one of the prophets.

15 He saith unto them, But whom say ye that I am?

16 And Simon Peter answered and said, Thou art the Christ, the Son of the living God.

17 And Jesus answered and said unto him, Blessed art thou, Simon Barjona: for flesh and blood hath not revealed it unto thee, but my Father which is in heaven.

18 And I say also unto thee, That thou art Peter, and upon this rock I will build my church; and the gates of hell shall not prevail against it.

19 And I will give unto thee the keys of the kingdom of heaven: and whatsoever thou shalt bind on earth shall be bound in heaven: and whatsoever thou shalt loose on earth shall be loosed in heaven.

20 Then charged he his disciples that they should tell no man that he was Jesus the Christ.

It's easy to tell someone to "Let It Go", but how can anyone simply let it go, or move past the pain.

This is how Jesus (Yeshua) makes it clear. Build your faith on a solid foundation, whereas the gates of Hell won't be able to prevail. Pray. Pray without ceasing. Don't put a moments thought into hesitating to pray - just do it. If you don't know how to pray. Simply say, "Lord, have mercy". It's a short and simple prayer, but it has proven to be most effective in all situations.

Whenever we place our full trust in our Father, His Son - Our Savior - there is no room for doubt, or fear. Because, by doing so, we've made a bold stance to lean not unto our own understanding, but willingly choose to acknowledge Him in all His ways. It says, I trust that the Father knows what's best for me. We accept that He is sovereign in all His ways.

Jeremiah 29: 11 King James Version (KJV)

11 For I know the thoughts that I think toward you, saith the Lord, thoughts of peace, and not of evil, to give you an expected end.

We need only trust in Our Heavenly Father. He sees all and knows all. But, I say to you, on this day, not as a Writer, but as a friend - forgive those who have wrought wickedness towards you. The day will come when the Sowers shall reap - on that day, ask God to have mercy on them - and yourselves. The fact that you're still here and still standing proves that God was with you. Although they tenaciously tried they did not prevail. God (Yahweh) allowed it, but didn't allow them to win.

CHAPTER 7

SELF REFLECTION

This is where we take a long hard look in the mirror - totally naked and bare faced. This is that moment when we must take responsibility for our own missteps and all the bull shiggidy we've put out there in the Universe. This is where we say, "Yeah, I did that - yes, I said that". This is where the rubber meets the road and we own up to our wicked behavior.

Listen, I know it's not easy to own up to your own bull shiggidy. Or, accept the fact that the earth doesn't revolve around you. We are not perfect, or innocent, or void of flaws. There are times when we don't dot every (I) or cross every (T). In some cases, we are the cause of the unfortunate circumstances happening to us. In some cases it's the things we say, do, or even don't do that bring about the mistreatment from others. Our tone, or callous responses can trigger unwanted reactions. Remember, for every action, there's a equal and opposite reaction.

But, if we're honest with ourselves and work on getting our own selves together - it leaves very little room to play victim, or sing the woe is me song. No one is exempt from the perils of life. Whenever we hold on to the past - we're subconsciously giving ourselves permission to stay stuck on go.

It's imperative that we take a look at who we really are and how we affect the people around us. Vibes don't lie. This includes our own energy. What type of energy are we putting into the atmosphere. Just like we can pick up on someone else's spirit, or energy. Other people can pick up on our vibes as well. If you're projecting a low countenance other people can sense that and act accordingly. If you're giving off wicked vibes, or being led by spiritual wickedness, people can feel that also. We don't have to ever speak a word for the people around us to know that something's not quite right.

We have to save ourselves first, before we can help somebody else.

Deuteronomy 32: 43

43 Rejoice, O ye nations, with his people: for he will avenge the blood of his servants, and will render vengeance to his adversaries, and will be merciful unto his land, and to his people

Learn from this and let it resonate in your soul. No one is exempt from facing their own karma - it's called sowing and reaping. Moses wasn't allowed to enter the Promise Land because of his transgressions against God (Yahweh). But, because of God's love for Moses, He allowed him to see it from the mountaintop before he died. Moses understood this and didn't hold any harsh feelings towards God. Why? Because, Moses reexamined his life - he took a long hard look in the mirror and saw himself for who he really was.

This is the same attitude we should be taking when we look into the mirror. And understandably so, not hold any grudges towards God, for being God.

God isn't a man that He should lie, or the son of man that He should repent.

CHAPTER 8

HEALING
FROM
WITHIN

Let's start with hugging ourselves. Forgiving ourselves for all the poor choices we've made along the way. Accepting that we're human and it's okay to be human - it's okay to have human emotions. It's okay to have flaws and not feel like we have to fit in. It's okay to be exactly who we are - the world needs us. The great part about being who we are is that there's no one in this great big old land like us - we are fearfully and wonderfully made. There are no other molds that can create another us - God threw the original mold away. We are unique, Baby - bought with a great price.

Whenever we grow to that place of forgiveness of self is when our lives take a turn in a more positive, peaceful and prosperous direction.

John 5 - 6 King *James Version (KJV)*

5 After this there was a feast of the Jews; and Jesus went up to Jerusalem.

2 Now there is at Jerusalem by the sheep market a pool, which is called in the Hebrew tongue Bethesda, having five porches.

3 In these lay a great multitude of impotent folk, of blind, halt, withered, waiting for the moving of the water.

4 For an angel went down at a certain season into the pool, and troubled the water: whosoever then first after the troubling of the water stepped in was made whole of whatsoever disease he had.

5 And a certain man was there, which had an infirmity thirty and eight years.

6 When Jesus saw him lie, and knew that he had been now a long time in that case, he saith unto him, Wilt thou be made whole?

7 The impotent man answered him, Sir, I have no man, when the water is troubled, to put me into the pool: but while I am coming, another steppeth down before me.

8 Jesus saith unto him, Rise, take up thy bed, and walk.

Healing is a process. It requires faith. It requires exile. It requires a deaf ear to outside influences. It requires being in the right place. Once it's achieved, it's our responsibility not to return back to the same behavior that took our health away.

Be Thou healed, and made whole.

Trust the process - and know that God's on your side.

CHAPTER 9

ONE DAY AT A TIME

This is a lesson many people struggle with. Especially, those who are constantly on the go for whatever reason. I must admit that I wrestle with this from time to time. It's a challenge to slow down when there seems to be so much to do. I'm learning how to politely say NO without regret. I'm teaching myself how to live in the moment and how to stop living in the future. Tomorrow isn't ours to give. Who are we to make plans for the future when our entire lives can be turned upside down in a twinkling of an eye. Life has this way of telling us that we are not the ones in control. Life doesn't suck - it's a beautiful thing to be a part of. It's how we live our lives, or the people we allow into our lives that's questionable and make for sucky moments.

But, when we relax - exhale - and simply let things be - that's when the real beauty of living begins. We have to give ourselves days when we're not tune into the world of technology. Unplugging from the world around us brings joy, love, peace - and clarity. Sometimes, we have to go into our "Secret Closet" and just be. Prayer, or Meditation in silence. Hiding ourselves away from the world around us will open up a whole new way of being, doing and thinking.

Even Jesus had to slip away for awhile to a quiet place and pray, or just be. Getting away from everything and everybody - even your precious Rugrats. Being in silence is like administering medicine to the soul. We are not any good to anyone if we don't take the time to recharge. We live in a society where everyone wants a piece of you. You're being pulled from both ends at home. You're being pulled at work - trying to juggle several projects at once. You're being pulled in every direction with errands and community efforts. It's no wonder that some people's health starts to fail them.

The problem with burning the candle at both ends is that eventually the light will go out. It's okay to keep yourself busy - because we all know that idle hands are the devil's workshop. However, when you forget to stop and smell the roses - your body will remind you that it needs rest. At this point, you're either going to the Emergency Room, or the Morgue.

Genesis 2: 2 -3 King James Version (*KJV*)

2 And on the seventh day God ended his work which he had made; and he rested on the seventh day from all his work which he had made.

3 And God blessed the seventh day, and sanctified it: because that in it he had rested from all his work which God created and made.

Matthew 11: 28 -30 King James Version (KJV)

28 Come unto me, all ye that labour and are heavy laden, and I will give you rest.

29 Take my yoke upon you, and learn of me; for I am meek and lowly in heart: and ye shall find rest unto your souls.

30 For my yoke is easy, and my burden is light.

Rest is needful. Even God, being Almighty, rested on the seventh day. Did He need to? Of course not. He's a spirit being. But, the lesson He is teaching is that rest does the body good. Having adequate amounts of sleep, or rest rejuvenates not only our mind, but the entire body.

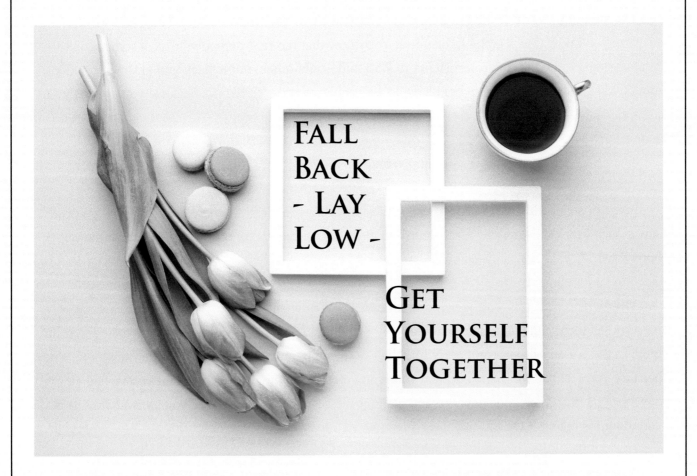

CHAPTER 10

FALL BACK - LAY LOW - GET YOURSELF TOGETHER

Sometimes, you've got to fall off the grid - get into your cubbie hole away from everybody and work on getting your life together. Working on goals that you've put off for far too long.

Learn how to make moves in silence. You don't have to broadcast everything that you're doing. It's no one's business and some of the people you're telling don't care. See, this is where a lot of people mess up their own blessings. By talking too much you can hinder your own progress.

You see it all the time, someone posting their next big adventure. They're all excited telling all of their followers about the great opportunities unfolding in their lives. Some of their friends are posting congratulations on their social media wall and others are patting them on the back (virtually speaking of course). For weeks all they seem to be talking about is how great things are coming along - even though the fan crowd has died down considerably.

Then it happens - this same person who has been singing and dancing in the rain like Gene Kelly for weeks starts posting about how everybody is a hater, how you can't trust anyone, how two faced so called friends are, or how everybody sucks and they're done with everything and everybody.

Crickets. Chirp Chirp.

The shiggidy has hit the fan and they are ready to blow. So you sit back, not saying a word, because you know this is going to be good. You know that the first person who says something to them is going to be lit into. You rush out to walk Fido right quick, come back and grab your popcorn and beverage - hoping that you don't have to pee in between the fireworks because you don't want to miss anything - sitting patiently waiting for the show to begin.

Then BAM!!! Like a bolt of lightning. There it is.

Some unsuspecting, sweet, kind, loss soul says, «Are you alright, what happened". All you can say is what Florida Evans said after returning from her husband's funeral when she threw the punch bowl down. D@## D@## D@##.

This person who was simply being kindhearted has now entered the Twilight Zone. You can literally see them clutching their phantom pearls and that one lone tear that refuses to drip down sits there in the corner of their right eye while their bottom lip quivers. You want to offer them a Kleenex because you feel bad for them, but then you remember this is the most excitement you've had all day - so you munch on your popcorn and wait for the comeback. Now, there you are watching this verbal tennis match. LOVE.

All of this could have been avoided if only they'd kept their mouth shut about their endeavors. There's nothing wrong with being excited about good news - but it's always best to hold your cards close to your chest until after the fact. What happened was, in the process of trying to take flight, someone came along trying to "help" and things went south real quick causing it all to crash.

Build your Empire in silence. When you keep quiet about what you're doing, people don't know which side to approach you on.

Psalm 46: 10 King James Version (KJV)

10 Be still, and know that I am God: I will be exalted among the heathen, I will be exalted in the earth.

Proverbs 17: 28 King James Version (KJV)

28 Even a fool, when he holdeth his peace, is counted wise: and he that shutteth his lips is esteemed a man of understanding.

In Conclusion:

What I have learned over the course of my years is that the one thing that remains consistent is that the power of love always wins in the end.

We can't choose our parents - we simply must play the hand we're dealt. And, although our lives may seem a bit sucky coming up, we have to eventually understand that there are no specific rules in this thing called Life. We just somehow have to muster a brave face and walk through it - even if we're terrified every step of the way. Sure, we are going to stumble and fall - but we will get back up. All days aren't going to be smooth sailing - but we'll manage somehow, because of the power that worketh in us. People will come and go in our lives - some for the better and some for the worse, but we will learn from those experiences and grow in grace one day at a time. No one is promised tomorrow - so we will learn how to live in the moment and not rush the future. For tomorrow will take care of itself - sufficient for today is the evil thereof. Let's not set ourselves in stone and become brutish and heartless because of those around us who walk in discord ever throwing darts. Instead, let's allow our light to shine so that others who are misinformed can see their way through the darkness.

In defense of parents all over the world - no one was given a handbook on how to raise children, it's something we learn along the way. There are no perfect parents, or stellar children - it is what it is. No one escapes this life without feeling the rain, or going through the storms.

"Even a flea can irritate a lion". ~Darius E. Frazier

I hope that this book has somehow helped you further grow. If nothing else, brought a little more understanding into your life and provided you moments of laughter. Laughter is medicine for the soul.

May you move forward in this thing called Life - prospering greatly on every turn.

"Rejection Is The New Blessing - Count It All Joy"

Dedication:

First, and far most, I give the Holy Trinity all the praise, honor and glory. God, The Father. Jesus, The Son. and The Holy Spirit.

I dedicate this book to those who have felt loss and misunderstood in their lives. To those who cry silently in the dark. To those who have felt constant rejection by people who didn't recognize their value. To those who struggle to fit into a world they were never meant to fit into because they are rare gems.

To my son, Darius E. Frazier

You are my rock and my greatest supporter. The day you were born I realized that God truly loved me to bless me with someone so amazing as you. Keep shinning your light, Son. You are a true Warrior and Friend.

My Fellow Support Team:

Devoe Frazier - Haynes
Lakesha Frazier - Johnson
Mia Irvin - Moore
Charlene Jones
JoAnne Jones - Smallwood
Rosa Mae Jones
Howar Dylette Hobbs - Davis
Micoya (Kia) Myers
Samelia Myers - Dickey
Nicole Myers
Yashika Myers
Adrian Williams
Frankie Keeling
Thelma Burse - Solomon
Jerolene Burse - Myers
Brenda - Burse Rollins
Kaynell Sneed - Bowman
Marinese Solomon
Ranji McMillan

Amani (Amani Jay) Jackson

Kyada M. Clarksmith

Ethelyn R. Solomon (A)

Enya Solomon

Phyllis Solomon -Brown

Willa A. Crook

Kawanza Alston

Chyneatha Burse

Johneatha Burse

Jonis Burse

Lesa Burse

Leila Burse

Takela Burse

Fredell Burse - McCord

Francine Black

Margaret Foster

Louvenia Jackson

Angela Smith

Willie Mae Lewis

Mary Alexander (Mary G)

Maxine Streeter

Angela M. Smith

Alma Schultz

Phyllis Ryan Stallworth

A very special thanks to Otis Myers, my beloved Uncle and Friend.

In Loving Memory of:

Jolie Jean Frazier

Willie Lee Frazier

Ricky L. Burse

Daisy B. Alston

Linda Alston

Ethlyn B. Burse

Rev. Eugene Burse

Sallye C. Burse

Michael Burse

Felton Burse Jr.

Bobby Stroud

Felton Burse

Abram Burse

John Burse

Eugene Burse Jr.

Printed in the United States
By Bookmasters